D1309930

J567.9 H159D
Halls, Kelly Milner.
Dinosaur parade

WITHDRAWN
FROM THE RECORDS OF THE
MID-CONTINENT PUBLIC LIBRARY

MID-CONTINENT PUBLIC LIBRARY
Oak Grove Branch
2320 S. Broadway Street
Oak Grove, MO 64075
OG

DINOSAUR PARADE

A Spectacle of Prehistoric Proportions

Kelly Milner Halls

Illustrated by
Rick C. Spears

LARK BOOKS
A Division of Sterling Publishing Co., Inc.
New York / London

Library of Congress Cataloging-in-Publication Data

Halls, Kelly Milner, 1957-
    Dinosaur parade / by Kelly Milner Halls ; illustrated by Rick C. Spears.
        p. cm.
    Includes index.
    ISBN-13: 978-1-60059-267-6 (hc-plc with jacket : alk. paper)
    ISBN-10: 1-60059-267-8 (hc-plc with jacket : alk. paper)
    1. Dinosaurs--Juvenile literature. I. Spears, Rick C. II. Title.
    QE861.5.H332 2008
    567.9--dc22
                            2007050677

MID-CONTINENT PUBLIC LIBRARY

3 0000 13066996 7

MID-CONTINENT PUBLIC LIBRARY
Oak Grove Branch
2320 S. Broadway Street
Oak Grove, MO 64075

OG

10 9 8 7 6 5 4 3 2 1

First Edition

Published by Lark Books, A Division of
Sterling Publishing Co., Inc.
387 Park Avenue South, New York, NY 10016

Text © 2008, Kelly Milner Halls
Illustrations © 2008, Rick C. Spears

Distributed in Canada by Sterling Publishing,
c/o Canadian Manda Group, 165 Dufferin Street
Toronto, Ontario, Canada M6K 3H6

Distributed in the United Kingdom by GMC Distribution Services,
Castle Place, 166 High Street, Lewes, East Sussex, England BN7 1XU

Distributed in Australia by Capricorn Link (Australia) Pty Ltd.,
P.O. Box 704, Windsor, NSW 2756 Australia

The written instructions, photographs, designs, patterns, and projects in this volume are intended for the personal use of
the reader and may be reproduced for that purpose only. Any other use, especially commercial use, is forbidden under law
without written permission of the copyright holder.

Every effort has been made to ensure that all the information in this book is accurate. However, due to differing conditions,
tools, and individual skills, the publisher cannot be responsible for any injuries, losses, and other damages that may result
from the use of the information in this book.

If you have questions or comments about this book, please contact:
Lark Books
67 Broadway
Asheville, NC 28801
828-253-0467

Manufactured in China

All rights reserved

ISBN 13: 978-1-60059-267-6

For information about custom editions, special sales, premium and corporate purchases, please contact Sterling Special Sales
Department at 800-805-5489 or specialsales@sterlingpub.com.

Dedication

To McLane Elementary School in
Olympia, Washington, and all little
dinosaur fans. Because you are as
important as big dinosaur fans—
in my book. *KMH*

To my niece, Jaclyn, who wasn't
born in time to be included
in my last dedication.

To Mom and Dad, for buying me
that first dinosaur book...now look
what you've done! *RCS*

Dinosaurs. How big? How small?
Sometimes we can't tell at all.

Here, then gone—so long ago
how they looked is hard to know.

So just for fun, we'll say they stayed
and joined a Dinosaur Parade.

Sauropods with necks so long,
were extra large and super strong.

broad footed

sauropods

SAWR-o-pods

Anchisaurus
(an-kee-SAWR-us)
"near lizard"
- 8 feet long (2.4 m)
- Early Jurassic
- Discovered in North America.
- Named in 1885.

Apatosaurus
(a-PAT-uh-SAWR-us)
"fake lizard"
- 80 feet long (24.4 m)
- Late Jurassic
- Discovered in North America.
- Named in 1877.

Camarasaurus
(CAM-uh-ra-SAWR-us)
"chamber lizard"

• 30 feet long (9.1 m)

• Late Jurassic

• Discovered in North America.

• Named in 1877.

Sauroposeidon
(SAWR-o-poe-SIDE-on)
"Poseidon's lizard"

• 100 feet long (30.5 m)

• Middle Cretaceous

• Discovered in North America.

• Named in 2000.

Saltasaurus
(SALT-uh-SAWR-us)
"lizard from Saltas"

• 40 feet long (12.2 m)

• Late Cretaceous

• Discovered in South America.

• Named in 1980.

Roaming free on ancient plains,
herds moved on, come sun or rain.

bird footed

ornithopods

OR-ni-tho-pods

Lesothosaurus
(le-SO-tho-SAWR-us)
"lizard from Lesotho"

- 3 feet long (0.9 m)
- Late Triassic
- Discovered in South Africa.
- Named in 1978.

Parasaurolophus
(pair-uh-SAWR-OL-uh-fus)
"crested lizard"

- 37 feet long (11.3 m)
- Late Cretaceous
- Discovered in North America.
- Named in 1922.

Edmontosaurus
(ed-MON-toe-SAWR-us)
"lizard from Edmonton"

• 42 feet long (12.8 m)

• Cretaceous

• Discovered in
North America.

• Named in 1917.

Camptosaurus
(CAMP-toe-SAWR-us)
"bent lizard"

• 20 feet long (6.1 m)

• Late Jurassic

• Discovered in
North America.

• Named in 1885.

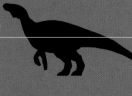

Iguanodon
(ig-WAN-a-don)
"Iguana toothed"

• 30 feet long (9.1 m)

• Early Cretaceous

• Discovered in
Great Britain.

• Named in 1881.

Some had frills, some had crests, all laid eggs in leafy nests.

more ornithopods

Hypsilophodon
(hip-si-LA-foe-don)
"high crested tooth"

- 5 feet long (1.5 m)
- Late Cretaceous
- Discovered in Europe.
- Named in 1869.

Maiasaura
(MY-a-SAWR-a)
"good mother lizard"

- 30 feet long (9.1 m)
- Cretaceous
- Discovered in North America.
- Named in 1979.

Lambeosaurus
(LAM-bee-o-SAWR-us)
"Lambe's lizard"

• 50 feet long (15.2 m)

• Late Cretaceous

• Discovered in
  North America.

• Named in 1923.

Lophorhothon
(LOW-for-HOE-thon)
"crested nose"

• 15 feet long (4.6 m)

• Late Cretaceous

• Discovered in
  North America.

• Named in 1960.

Corythosaurus
(co-REETH-o-SAWR-us)
"helmet lizard"

• 33 feet long (10.1 m)

• Cretaceous

• Discovered in
  North America.

• Named in 1914.

When banging noggins was the rule, fancy skulls made hard heads cool.

thick headed lizards

pachycephalosaurs

pack-ee-SEF-a-low-sawrs

Wannanosaurus
(wah-NAN-o-SAWR-us)
"lizard from Wannan"

- 39 inches long (99.1 cm)
- Late Cretaceous
- Discovered in Asia.
- Named in 1977.

Stygimoloch
(STIG-ee-MO-lock)
"demon from the river Styx"

- 8½ feet long (2.6 m)
- Late Cretaceous
- Discovered in North America.
- Named in 1983.

Homalocephale
(home-a-low-SEF-a-lee)
"level head"

- 5 feet long (1.5 m)
- Late Cretaceous
- Discovered in Mongolia.
- Named in 1974.

Pachycephalosaurus
(pak-ee-SEF-a-low-SAWR-us)
"thick headed lizard"

- 15 feet long (4.6 m)
- Late Cretaceous
- Discovered in North America.
- Named in 1943.

Stegoceras
(steg-OSS-er-as)
"roofed horn"

- 7 feet long (2.1 m)
- Late Cretaceous
- Discovered in North America.
- Named in 1902.

Armored dinos dazzled mates with bumps and scutes, spikes and plates.

shield bearers

thyreophorans

THY-ree-o-FOR-ans

Scutellosaurus
(SCU-tuh-luh-SAWR-us)
"little shielded lizard"

- 4 feet long (1.2 m)
- Early Jurassic
- Discovered in North America.
- Named in 1981.

Stegosaurus
(STEG-o-SAWR-us)
"roof lizard"

- 30 feet long (9.1 m)
- Late Jurassic
- Discovered in North America.
- Named in 1877.

Nodosaurus	**Ankylosaurus**	**Polacanthus**
(no-do-SAWR-us)	(an-KY-lo-SAWR-us)	(pole-a-CAN-thus)
"knobbed lizard"	"stiffened lizard"	"many thorns"
• 15 feet long (4.6 m)	• 29 feet long (8.8 m)	• 15 feet long (4.6 m)
• Early Cretaceous	• Late Cretaceous	• Early Cretaceous
• Discovered in North America.	• Discovered in North America.	• Discovered in England.
• Named in 1889.	• Named in 1908.	• Named in 1865.

Horns adorned some grazing beasts as they moved from feast to feast.

horn faced

ceratopsians

sar-a-TOP-see-ans

Leptoceratops
(LEP-toe-SER-uh-tops)
"slender horned face"

- 6½ feet long (2 m)
- Late Cretaceous
- Discovered in North America.
- Named in 1914.

Triceratops
(tri-SER-uh-tops)
"three horned face"

- 30 feet long (9.1 m)
- Late Cretaceous
- Discovered in North America.
- Named in 1889.

Psittacosaurus
(sit-TAK-uh-SAWR-us)
"parrot lizard"
- 5 feet long (1.5 m)
- Cretaceous
- Discovered in Asia.
- Named in 1923.

Protoceratops
(pro-toe-SER-uh-tops)
"first horned face"
- 7 feet long (2.1 m)
- Late Cretaceous
- Discovered in Asia.
- Named in 1923.

Styracosaurus
(sty-RAK-uh-SAWR-us)
"spiked lizard"
- 18 feet long (5.5 m)
- Late Cretaceous
- Discovered in North America.
- Named in 1913.

Tough and strong in peace or war,
"Stay away," they seemed to roar.

more ceratopsians

Bagaceratops
(bag-a-SER-a-tops)
"small horned faced"

- 3 feet long (0.9 m)
- Late Cretaceous
- Discovered in Mongolia.
- Named in 1975.

Einiosaurus
(EYE-nee-o-SAWR-us)
"buffalo lizard"

- 20 feet long (6.1 m)
- Cretaceous
- Discovered in North America.
- Named in 1995.

Chasmosaurus
(CAZ-moe-SAWR-us)
"opening lizard"
- 26 feet long (7.9 m)
- Cretaceous
- Discovered in North America.
- Named in 1914.

Pachyrhinosaurus
(PACK-ee-rye-no-SAWR-us)
"thick nosed reptile"
- 20 feet long (6.1 m)
- Late Cretaceous
- Discovered in North America.
- Named in 1950.

Montanoceratops
(mon-TAN-o-SER-a-tops)
"horned faced from Montana"
- 6 feet long (1.8 m)
- Cretaceous
- Discovered in North America.
- Named in 1951.

Fast and smart like modern birds, these dinosaurs survived in herds.

bird mimics

ornithomimosaurs

OR-ni-tho-MIME-o-sawrs

Ornitholestes
(OR-ni-tho-LEES-tess)
"bird robber"
- 6 feet long (1.8 m)
- Late Jurassic
- Discovered in North America.
- Named in 1903.

Ornithomimus
(OR-ni-tho-MIME-us)
"bird mimic"
- 15 feet long (4.6 m)
- Late Cretaceous
- Discovered in North America.
- Named in 1890.

Gallimimus
(gal-i-MIME-us)
"rooster mimic"
• 17 feet long (5.2 m)
• Late Cretaceous
• Discovered in China.
• Named in 1972.

Struthiomimus
(struth-ee-o-MIME-us)
"ostrich mimic"
• 13 feet long (4 m)
• Late Cretaceous
• Discovered in North America.
• Named in 1917.

Pelicanimimus
(pel-a-CAN-I-mime-us)
"pelican mimic"
• 6½ feet long (2 m)
• Early Cretaceous
• Discovered in Spain.
• Named in 1994.

Raptors ran on feet with claws, eating meat with toothy jaws.

swift lizards

dromaeosaurs

droe-MAY-o-sawrs

Microraptor
(MY-crow-RAP-tor)
"small robber"

• 16 inches long (40.6 cm)

• Early Cretaceous

• Discovered in Asia.

• Named in 2000.

Megaraptor
(MEG-uh-RAP-tor)
"giant robber"

• 25 feet long (7.6 m)

• Late Cretaceous

• Discovered in South America.

• Named in 1998.

Oviraptor
(O-ve-RAP-tor)
"egg robber"
- 7 feet long (2.1 m)
- Late Cretaceous
- Discovered in Asia.
- Named in 1924.

Velociraptor
(ve-LAW-si-RAP-tor)
"swift robber"
- 5½ feet long (1.7 m)
- Late Cretaceous
- Discovered in Asia.
- Named in 1924.

Utahraptor
(U-ta-RAP-tor)
"Utah robber"
- 20 feet long (6.1 m)
- Cretaceous
- Discovered in North America.
- Named in 1993.

Theropods once ruled the day, and T. rex was the king, they say.

beast footed

theropods

THER-o-pods

Carnotaurus
(carn-o-TAWR-us)
"flesh eating bull"

- 25 feet long (7.6 m)
- Cretaceous
- Discovered in South America.
- Named in 1985.

Tyrannosaurus rex
(tie-RAN-o-SAWR-us rex)
"lizard king"

- 40 feet long (12.2 m)
- Late Cretaceous
- Discovered in North America.
- Named in 1905.

Compsognathus
(comp-sog-NAY-thus)
"dainty jaw"
- 3 feet long (0.9 m)
- Late Jurassic
- Discovered in France.
- Named in 1859.

Eotyrannus
(EE-o-tie-RAN-us)
"dawn tyrant"
- 15 feet long (4.6 m)
- Middle Cretaceous
- Discovered in Great Britain.
- Named in 2001.

Allosaurus
(AL-o-SAWR-us)
"different lizard"
- 30 feet long (9.1 m)
- Late Jurassic
- Discovered in North America.
- Named in 1877.

Carving teeth, a keen sense of smell kept these bipeds eating well.

more theropods

Cryolophosaurus
(cry-o-LOAF-o-SAWR-us)
"frozen crested lizard"

- 20 feet long (6.1 m)
- Jurassic
- Discovered in Antarctica.
- Named in 1994.

Spinosaurus
(SPY-no-SAWR-us)
"spine lizard"

- 59 feet long (18 m)
- Cretaceous
- Discovered in Egypt.
- Named in 1915.

Coelophysis
(see-low-FIE-sis)
"hollow form"

- 10 feet long (3 m)
- Middle Triassic
- Discovered in North America.
- Named in 1889.

Ceratosaurus
(ser-AT-o-SAWR-us)
"horned lizard"

- 30 feet long (9.1 m)
- Late Jurassic
- Discovered in North America.
- Named in 1884.

Eoraptor
(ee-o-RAP-tor)
"dawn plunderer"

- 3 feet long (0.9 m)
- Late Triassic
- Discovered in Argentina.
- Named in 1993.

Lengthy claws, no taste for meat,
Therizinosaurs had plants to eat.

cutting lizards

therizinosaurs

ther-uh-ZEEN-o-sawrs

Beipiaosaurus
(bay-pyow-SAWR-us)
"lizard from Beipiao"
- 7 feet long (2.1 m)
- Cretaceous
- Discovered in China.
- Named in 1999.

Alxasaurus
(AL-shuh-SAWR-us)
"lizard from Alxa"
- 13 feet long (4 m)
- Early Cretaceous
- Discovered in Mongolia.
- Named in 1993.

Segnosaurus
(seg-no-SAWR-us)
"slow lizard"
- 19 feet long (5.8 m)
- Cretaceous
- Discovered in Mongolia.
- Named in 1979.

Therizinosaurus
(there-uh-ZEEN-o-SAWR-us)
"scythe lizard"
- 26 feet long (7.9 m)
- Late Cretaceous
- Discovered in Mongolia.
- Named in 1954.

Falcarius
(fall-CARE-ee-us)
"sickle maker"
- 13 feet long (4 m)
- Early Cretaceous
- Discovered in North America.
- Named in 2005.

Natural causes wiped them out
long before kids walked about.

Rocky bones now on display
make us long for distant days.

PALEO-FLYER

Mini homo sapiens
(min-ee ho-mo SAY-pee-ens)
"small wise men"

• 3½ feet tall (1.1 m)

• 200,000 years ago
to present.

• Found worldwide.

But dino dreams need never fade, just join the Dinosaur Parade!

Dracorex hogwartsia
(DRAY-co-REX hog-WART-see-ah)
"dragon king of Hogwarts"

• 10 feet long (3 m)

• Late Cretaceous

• Discovered in North America.

• Named in 2002.

Paleontologist
(pay-LEE-on-TOL-o-gist)
"dinosaur scientist"

• Size varies

• Term first used in 1830.

About the Dinosaurs in the Dinosaur Parade

Sauropods were plant-eaters. Like modern birds, most of them swallowed stones to help digest their food. Sauropods have been found on every continent except Antarctica. *Anchisaurus* was one of the first dinosaurs found in the USA.

Ornithopods were plant-eaters. Most had three toes on their feet, like modern birds, but some had four. Some ornithopods, like *Parasaurolophus*, may have made sounds with their crests (the decorative parts on top of their heads).

Pachycephalosaurs were plant-eaters. Male pachycephalosaurs probably banged their heads into each other's hind ends to prove they were tough. The winners got the girls. *Stegoceras'* heads grew thicker and wider as they got older.

Thyreophorans were plant-eaters. Their armor protected them from predators. It probably helped them recognize each other, too. *Ankylosaurus* could shatter bones with its clubbed tail.

Ceratopsians were plant-eaters. They probably lived in herds. Some had horns on their heads to attract mates and battle predators. Most ceratopsians ran on four legs, but *Leptoceratops* ran on two.

Ornithomimosaurs ate both plants and meat. Most ornithomimosaurs looked like modern-day ostriches. They also ran very quickly. *Struthiomimus* may have been able to run as fast as 50 miles (80.5 km) per hour.

Dromaeosaurs were meat-eaters. Some had long claws that they used to slash their prey. *Megaraptor's* claw was 13 inches (33 cm) long! Dromaeosaurs probably hunted in packs, taking down dinosaurs much bigger than they were.

Theropods were meat-eaters. They had a keen sense of smell, so some may have been scavengers. *Eoraptor*, one of the oldest dinosaurs found so far, is a theropod. *Tyrannosaurus rex,* a theropod, is one of the most popular dinosaurs of all time.

Therizinosaurs were plant-eaters. But they may have also eaten insects. *Alxasaurus* and other therizinosaurs used long claws to dig for roots and even termites. *Beipiaosaurus* may have had soft, fluffy feathers like a molting bird.

All of the dinosaurs lived during the Mesozoic Era, but many of them lived millions of years apart! The Mesozoic Era was divided into three different periods: the Triassic (245 to 208 million years ago), the Jurassic (208 to 146 million years ago), and the Cretaceous (146 to 65 million years ago).

Paleontologists take a little while to make sure that the fossils they've found belong to a brand new type of dinosaur. When all the scientists agree, the new dinosaur gets its own name!

Every time a new fossil is found, we learn more about the fascinating creatures that lived so long ago. There's more left to discover—in other books and buried in stone.